YOUNG EUROPEAN
FASHION
DESIGNERS

daab

Introduction 4

INTRODUCTION

Fashion is a prevailing trend, an expression and precursor of societal developments. It reflects not only how humans currently live but also makes clear what is yet to come. This book presents a new generation of designers that have today made an impact on the future of fashion. They are not only creating the look of the times, but also have a profound influence on what soon will happen in fashion. The „Young European Fashion Designers" presented in this book stand for innovation and courage. They experiment with unconventional forms as well as with eclectic color and material combinations and thus produce completely new looks.

Long ago, the young creative folk began to challenge the traditional messages of clothing. The variety of ethnic and sub-cultural influences changed their view of the definition of fashion up to now and broadened the horizon for new possibilities. The young designers find other ways to present and offer fashion. Yet they remain true to themselves and their individual style. Their visions are not guided primarily by materialistic interests rather are the expression of creative freedom. They focus on the topic of individualism. And as a trend, that will become an ever increasing quality in the era of mass production.

The „Young European Fashion Designers" presented here distance themselves from the conventional methods of fashion statement. Instead of traditional fashion shows they often surprise us with innovative forms of presentation: they make films or stage performances and installations that remove the barriers between conceptual art and fashion. They are also breaking new ground with regard to sales. Many of the „Young European Fashion Designers" offer fashion online instead of in boutiques or department stores as we are accustomed to. Modern communications make fashion design today possible in many different locations – even great distances from the large fashion metropolises and fashion shows. Modern communications also relieve the young designers of the research in order for them to find their inspirations all over the world.

Since Europe has become united, the national borders are falling away. The differing cultural styles, influences, and the behavior of society are coming together. This book presents fashion designers of varying directions from numerous European countries. The new generation of designers is spread across the entire continent and are not found only in the large fashion centers. Therefore, it is sometimes worthwhile to look away from the traditional fashion metropolises to the new centers of creativity. Not only the famous designers from Paris, London, and Milan are making an impression on stylish diversity. Many of the national capitals such as Copenhagen, Barcelona or Berlin now have a lively fashion scene that is developing quickly.

This book illustrates the style of each of the designers in brilliant color photos that document a wide variety of earlier and current pieces from their collections, look book excerpts, catwalk and campaign scenes. Small portraits introduce the fashion designer as personalities with their respective philosophy and manner of working. It is the risk they all have undertaken together in the unforgiving business of fashion; nevertheless, they have been able to draw attention to themselves despite an enormous amount of competition.

It is admirable how consequential and willful all these „Young European Fashion Designers" are and how they are able to convert their ideas into a philosophy which gave a characteristic, recognition factor to the label. And it is remarkable how many variants of fashion design and its realization there are which – despite the claim that everything in the fashion industry has been done before – never seems boring.

Mode ist eine Zeitströmung, ein Ausdruck und Vorbote gesellschaftlicher Entwicklungen. Sie spiegelt nicht nur wieder, wie der Mensch gerade lebt, sondern macht auch sichtbar, was kommen wird. Das vorliegende Buch präsentiert eine neue Generation von Designern, die bereits heute die Zukunft der Mode prägt. Sie kreiert nicht nur den Look der Zeit, sondern beeinflusst tief greifend auch das, was schon bald in der Mode passieren wird. Die in diesem Buch präsentierten „Young European Fashion Designers" stehen für Innovation und Mut. Sie experimentieren mit unkonventionellen Formen sowie vielseitigen Farb- und Stoffkombinationen und bringen so neue Erscheinungsbilder hervor.

Längst haben die jungen Kreativen begonnen, die traditionellen Botschaften von Kleidung in Frage zu stellen. Die Vielfalt ethnischer und subkultureller Einflüsse verzerrt ihren Blick auf die bisherige Definition von Mode und öffnet den Horizont für neue Möglichkeiten. Die jungen Designer finden andere Wege, Mode zu präsentieren und anzubieten. Dabei bleiben sie sich und ihrem individuellen Stil treu. Ihre Visionen werden nicht in erster Linie durch konsumorientierte Interessen gelenkt, sondern sind Ausdruck der gestalterischen Freiheit. Sie stellen das Thema Individualismus in den Mittelpunkt. Und das wird zu Zeiten der Massenproduktion immer mehr als Trend an Wert gewinnen.
Die hier vorgestellten „Young European Fashion Designers" lösen sich von den konventionellen Methoden der Modedarstellung. Statt traditioneller Modenschauen überraschen sie oft mit neuartigen Präsentationsformen: Sie machen Filme oder inszenieren Vorführungen und Installationen, die die Grenzen zwischen konzeptioneller Kunst und Mode aufheben. Auch im Verkauf gehen sie neue Wege. Viele der „Young European Fashion Designers" bieten ihre Mode online an, statt wie gewohnt in Boutiquen oder Kaufhäusern. Die moderne Kommunikation macht Modedesign heute an vielen Orten möglich – auch weitab der großen Modemetropolen und Modemessen. Sie erleichtert den jungen Designern die Recherche, so dass sie ihre Inspirationen überall auf der Welt finden können.
Mit dem vereinigten Europa verschwimmen die Landesgrenzen. Die unterschiedlichen kulturellen Stile, Einflüsse und das Verhalten der Gesellschaft nähern sich einander an. Das Buch präsentiert Modedesigner verschiedenster Richtungen aus vielen europäischen Ländern. Die neue Designer-Generation ist über den ganzen Kontinent verstreut und nicht nur in den großen Modezentren zu finden. Daher lohnt es sich, bisweilen den Blick von den traditionellen Modemetropolen in die neuen Zentren der Kreativität zu lenken. Nicht nur die großen Designer aus Paris, London und Mailand prägen die modische Vielfalt. Viele Hauptstädte wie Kopenhagen, Barcelona oder Berlin haben mittlerweile eine lebhafte Modeszene, die sich rasant entwickelt.

Das Buch bildet den Stil eines jeden Designers durch brillante Farbfotos ab, die eine große Vielfalt von früheren und aktuellen Kollektionsteilen, Lookbook-Auszügen, Catwalk- und Kampagnenszenen dokumentieren. Kleine Portraits stellen die Modedesigner als Persönlichkeiten mit ihrer jeweiligen Philosophie und Arbeitsweise vor. Ihnen gemeinsam ist das Risiko, dem sie sich im harten Modebusiness gestellt haben, und die Aufmerksamkeit, die sie trotz der enormen Konkurrenz auf sich lenken konnten.

Es ist bewundernswert, wie konsequent und eigenwillig alle diese „Young European Fashion Designers" ihre Ideen in eine Philosophie umsetzen konnten, die dem Label einen charakteristischen Wiedererkennungswert verleihen konnte. Und es ist bemerkenswert, wie viele Varianten von Modedesign und seiner Realisierung es gibt, die – trotz der Behauptung, dass es in der Mode alles schon einmal gegeben hat – nie langweilig wirken.

La moda es una tendencia que expresa y anticipa desarrollos sociales. No solamente refleja cómo vive el hombre en la actualidad, sino que también muestra lo que vendrá. Este libro presenta una nueva generación de diseñadores que está marcando hoy el futuro de la moda. Una generación que crea no solamente el estilo actual, sino que también influye profundamente en lo que ocurrirá en la moda en el futuro. Los "Young European Fashion Designers" presentados en este libro son un símbolo de innovación y osadía. Experimentan con formas no convencionales, así como con combinaciones de colores y materiales, planteando una imagen totalmente renovada.

Hace ya tiempo que los jóvenes creativos empezaron a cuestionar los mensajes tradicionales de la vestimenta. La variedad de influencias étnicas y subculturales distorsiona su mirada sobre la definición de la moda según se la conoce y abre el horizonte para nuevas posibilidades. Los diseñadores jóvenes encuentran maneras diferentes de presentar y ofrecer la moda, manteniéndose siempre fieles a sí mismos y a su estilo individual. Sus visiones no están motivadas en primer lugar por intereses orientados al consumo, sino que son una expresión de la libre creatividad. Colocan en el centro el tema del individualismo. Esta tendencia, en plena época de la producción en masa, cobrará cada vez más valor.

Los jóvenes diseñadores de moda europeos presentados en este volumen se han liberado de los métodos convencionales de representación de la moda. En lugar de los tradicionales desfiles, suelen sorprender con nuevas formas de presentación: filman películas o diseñan presentaciones e instalaciones que borran los límites entre el arte conceptual y la moda. También transitan nuevos caminos en el campo de las ventas; muchos de los "Young European Fashion Designers" ofrecen sus diseños en la red, en vez de en las boutiques o centros de compra tradicionales. Los medios modernos de comunicación llevan el diseño de moda a muchos lugares, incluso muchos alejados de las grandes metrópolis o ferias de la moda. La comunicación también facilita el trabajo de investigación de los diseñadores jóvenes, quienes pueden encontrar inspiración en cualquier lugar del mundo.

Con la Europa unida desaparecen los límites entre los países. Los diferentes estilos culturales, influencias y comportamientos sociales se van acercando unos a otros. Este libro presenta diseñadores de moda con las orientaciones más diferentes, provenientes de numerosos países europeos. La nueva generación de diseñadores está dispersa por todo el continente y no solamente en los centros de la moda. Por ello vale la pena mirar más allá de las metrópolis tradicionales de la moda, hacia los nuevos centros de creatividad. No solamente los grandes diseñadores de París, Londres y Milán marcan la diversidad de la moda. Muchas ciudades como Copenhague, Barcelona o Berlín tienen actualmente una vida muy rica (y de desarrollo muy veloz) en términos del diseño de moda.

Este libro ilustra el estilo de cada diseñador por medio de excelentes fotografías en color que documentan una gran variedad de piezas de colecciones pasadas y actuales, fotos tomadas de lookbooks o catálogos de imágenes, escenas de los desfiles de moda o de campañas publicitarias. Breves textos presentan a los diseñadores, sus personalidades, filosofías y formas de trabajo. Lo que tienen en común es el riesgo que han tomado para abrirse camino en el duro mundo del negocio de la moda y la atención que han podido lograr a pesar de la enorme competencia que allí reina.

Resulta admirable con qué coherencia y voluntad todos estos jóvenes han logrado traducir sus ideas en una filosofía que le da a cada marca una característica única y reconocible. Y se debe destacar cuántas variantes del diseño de la moda y su realización existen que, a pesar de que siempre se dice que en la moda ya se hizo todo alguna vez, nunca resultan aburridas.

La mode est une tendance qui exprime et anticipe les évolutions sociales. Elle reflète non seulement la manière dont l'homme vit actuellement, mais elle montre aussi ce qui va se produire. Cet ouvrage présente une nouvelle génération de créateurs qui marquent déjà l'avenir de la mode. Une génération qui crée non seulement le style actuel mais influence aussi profondément ce qui va bientôt se passer dans la mode à l'avenir. Les „Young European Fashion Designers" présentés dans cet ouvrage sont un symbole d'innovation et de courage. Ils expérimentent avec des formes non conventionnelles tout comme avec de nombreuses combinaisons de couleurs et de matériaux, créant ainsi des images entièrement neuves.

Ces jeunes créateurs ont commencé il y a longtemps déjà à remettre en question les messages traditionnels de l'habillement. La variété des influences ethniques et subculturelles déforme leur vision de la définition de la mode jusqu'ici utilisée et leur ouvre l'horizon sur de nouvelles possibilités. Les jeunes créateurs trouvent d'autres manières de présenter et de proposer leur mode tout en restant fidèles à eux-mêmes et à leur style personnel. Leurs visions ne sont pas motivées en premier lieu par des intérêts économiques de consommation, elles sont l'expression d'une certaine liberté de création. Elles placent au centre le thème de l'individualisme et cette tendance, en pleine époque de la production en masse, acquerra une valeur en plus en plus importante.

Les „Young European Fashion Designers" ici présentés se détachent des méthodes conventionnelles de représentation de la mode. Au lieu des défilés de mode traditionnels, ils surprennent souvent par de nouvelles formes de présentation : ils font des films ou conçoivent des présentations et des installations qui abolissent les frontières entre l'art conceptuel et la mode. Dans la vente également, ils empruntent de nouvelles voies. De nombreux „Young European Fashion Designers" proposent souvent leur mode sur Internet au lieu de la vendre comme cela se fait habituellement dans les boutiques et les grands magasins. La communication moderne permet la création de mode en de nombreux lieux aujourd'hui – même loin des grandes métropoles de la mode et autres salons importants. Elle facilite également le travail d'investigation des jeunes créateurs qui peuvent alors trouver leur inspiration partout à travers le monde.

Avec l'Europe unie, les frontières entre les pays disparaissent. Les différents styles culturels, mais aussi les influences et les comportements sociaux se rapprochent les uns des autres. L'ouvrage présente des créateurs de mode d'orientations très différentes venant de nombreux pays européens. La nouvelle génération de créateurs est dispersée sur tout le continent et pas seulement dans les grands centres de la mode. C'est la raison pour laquelle il est important de regarder de temps en temps au-delà des métropoles traditionnelles de la mode vers les nouveaux centres de création. Les grands créateurs de Paris, Londres et Milan ne sont pas les seuls à contribuer à la variété de la mode. De nombreuses grandes villes comme Copenhague, Barcelone ou Berlin sont désormais des centres vivants de la mode qui se développent à une allure foudroyante.

L'ouvrage présente le style de chaque créateur grâce à d'excellentes photos en couleurs qui documentent la grande variété de pièces de collection d'aujourd'hui et d'autrefois, d'extraits de lookbooks, de scènes de défilés de mode et de campagnes publicitaires. De petits portraits présentent les créateurs de mode, leur personnalité, leur philosophie et leur méthode de travail. Ils ont en commun le risque qu'ils ont pris pour s'imposer dans le monde dur de la mode et l'intérêt qu'ils ont réussi à susciter pour leur création en dépit de l'énorme concurrence qui règne dans ce domaine.

La manière conséquente et volontaire dont tous ces „Young European Fashion Designers" ont réussi à traduire leurs idées en une philosophie qui donne à chaque marque un caractère unique et reconnaissable, est remarquable. Il faut souligner également le nombre incroyable de variantes du design et de sa réalisation qui – même si l'on dit sans cesse que l'on a déjà tout vu dans la mode – ne sont jamais ennuyeuses.

La moda rappresenta una corrente del tempo, un'espressione ed un antesignano degli sviluppi sociali. Essa rispecchia, non solo il modo di vita attuale dell'individuo, ma anche rende presumibile ciò che verrà. Questo libro presenta una nuova generazione di stilisti che segnano già oggi il futuro della moda. Questa generazione realizza il Look attuale, ma influenza profondamente anche ciò che succederà presto in questo settore. Gli „Young European Fashion Designers" presentati in questo libro si distinguono per il loro spirito innovativo e per la loro voglia di osare. Sperimentano attraverso forme non convenzionali, utilizzando combinazioni diverse sia cromatiche sia di tessuti: fanno nascere così nuove concezioni espressive.

Da molto tempo, i giovani stilisti hanno iniziato a mettere in discussione i messaggi tradizionali provenienti dall'abbigliamento. L'eccezionale molteplicità di influssi etnici ed interculturali modifica la loro definizione della moda finora valida e considera nuovi orizzonti, caratterizzati da nuove possibilità. I giovani stilisti trovano altri metodi di presentare ed offrire la moda. Facendo questo, restano però fedeli a loro stessi ed al loro stile individuale. Le loro concezioni non sono determinate in prima linea dagli interessi dettati dai consumatori, bensì si configurano come espressione della loro libertà creativa. Il concetto di individualismo diventa così prioritario. E questo acquista sempre più valore come tendenza, in un periodo contrassegnato dalla produzione in massa.

Gli „Young European Fashion Designers" qui presentati rifiutano i metodi convenzionali della rappresentazione della moda. Invece delle consuete sfilate, essi sorprendono utilizzando nuove metodologie per rendere note le loro creazioni: realizzano filmati o inscenano dimostrazioni ed installazioni che annullano il divario tra l'arte concettuale e la moda. Anche per la vendita essi adottano metodi nuovi: molti degli „Young European Fashion Designers" offrono le loro creazioni on-line, invece di utilizzare delle normali boutiques o degli fashion-stores. Le tipologie moderne di comunicazione rende possibile la creazione di capi-moda in molti luoghi – anche molto distanti dalle grandi metropoli della moda e dalle fiere dell'abbigliamento. La globalizzazione facilita la ricerca ai nuovi stilisti, affinché possano trovare ispirazione ovunque nel mondo.

Grazie all'Europa Unita, i confini nazionali sono diventati più labili. I diversi stili culturali, le diverse influenze ed il comportamento della società sono sempre più simili e più vicini. Il libro presenta degli stilisti di moda di diversi orientamenti e provenienti da molti Paesi europei diversi. La nuova generazione di Designer si esprime nell'intero continente e non solo nei grandi ed affermati centri della moda. perciò vale la pena di volgere lo sguardo dalle metropoli della moda tradizionali ai nuovi centri della creatività. Non solo i grandi stilisti di Parigi, Londra e Milano influenzano le diverse tendenze moda. Molte capitali, come Copenhagen, Barcellona o Berlino godono già di una cultura della moda molto viva ed in continua evoluzione.

Il libro illustra lo stile di ogni stilista, attraverso eccezionali foto a colori che documentano l'enorme molteplicità dei capi di collezione precedenti ed attuali, estratti dei Lookbook, immagini ricavate dalle passerelle e dalle promozioni. Si tratta di piccoli ritratti che presentano i giovani stilisti come personalità contraddistinte ognuna dalla propria filosofia e metodologia di lavoro. Le caratteristiche comuni per tutti loro sono, da una parte, il rischio di lavorare nel difficile fashion-business e dall'altra, l'attenzione che si sono meritati, nonostante l'enorme concorrenza.

È sorprendente come tutti questi „Young European Fashion Designers" abbiano potuto applicare in modo coerente e caparbio le loro idee, nell'elaborazione di una filosofia che arricchisce il marchio con un valore di riconoscimento caratteristico. Ed è altresì ammirevole osservare quante varianti di fashion-design vi sono, insieme alla loro relativa realizzazione, la quale – nonostante si creda che nella moda si sia già visto tutto – non è invece mai noiosa.

A&V | VILNIUS
Alex Pogrebnojus, Vida Simanaviciute

Established in 1993 by Alex Pogrebnojus and Vida Simanaviciute, the studio is based in Vilnius, Lithuania. The
designers present two seasonal collections per year and
also undertake individual commissions as well as costume
design for theatre performances.
Pogrebnojus (born in 1968) studied theatre direction at Vilnius Conservatoire (1989-1992) while Simanaviciute (born
in 1961) studied design at Kaunas Art School (1984-1988).
What is first apparent from their collections is the harmony
of colours, form and mood. Looking deeper, the undoubted
experience, professionalism, and restless creativity is hard
to define in words but can be sensed instantly. There is a
desire to look at the clothes because they are so pleas-
ing to the eye; to touch them because the body longs for
new experiences; and to be the one for whom these clothes
have been designed. Moments of life are miscellaneous and
unpredictable, just like every detail of A&V's clothes.

www.lithill.lt/a&v

1 spring summer 2006
2 spring summer 2007
3 fall winter 2006/07

Photos: PIX studjia (3), Modestas Ezerskis (1, 2)

1

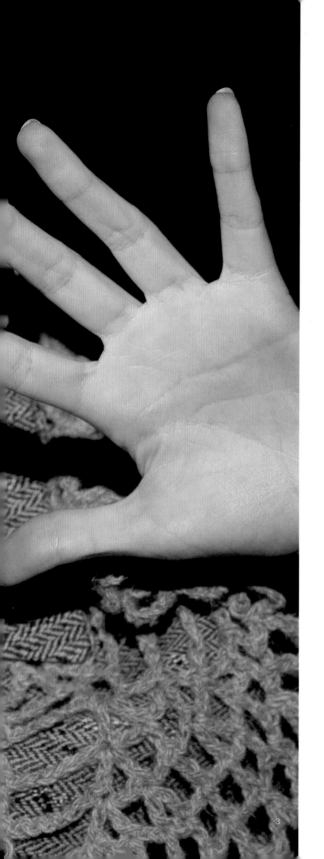

AIMEE MCWILLIAMS | LONDON
Aimee McWilliams

Among the UK's most successful rising designers, Aimee McWilliams graduated from Central Saint Martins College of Art and Design, London, winning the L'Oreal Total Look award for the best collection. She has since received job opportunities from industry names such as Roberto Cavalli, John Galliano and Gianfranco Ferre as well as retail accounts at the Di Milo's boutique in Harrods and online at brittique.com. Her work is distinguished by exquisite finishing and a unique approach to cutting. Subtle flamboyance combined with uncompromised wearability has earned McWilliams the accolade of an avante-garde designer with an air of eccentricity.
Regular media coverage ranges from British and Italian Vogue, to projects for MTV and The Clothes Show. She recently won a commission from stylists to The Rolling Stones and been nominated for Scottish Designer of the year. Her unique collections are presented at the On/Off schedule at the Royal Academy of Art during London Fashion Week.

www.aimeemcwilliams.com

spring summer 2007

Photos: Chris Moore

ALEXANDRA MOURA | LISBON
Alexandra Moura

Born in Lisbon in 1973, Alexandra Moura trained in fashion at IADE and has since participated in various fashion events such as The National Young Designers Show, when she was selected to represent Portugal in the first biannual "Portuguese Speaking Countries Young Designers" fashion event in Cabo Verde. From 1997-2001 she worked for Portuguese designers Ana Salazar and José António Tenente.

In 2000 she was invited by Novos Talentos/Optimus (New Talents) to present her first major solo collection in Lisbon and continues to show her work twice yearly at Lisbon Fashion Week. Her collections have featured in Barcelona's Bread & Butter shows (2006 and 2007), in Berlin at the Baltic-Sea Hi Fashion event (2005), and in Brazil at Dragão Fashion Week. Her work has appeared on Portuguese stamps, as staff uniforms at Atlantis Corporation stores, and adorning leading vocalists Sonia Tavares and Teresa Salgueiro. She recently presented her summer 2007 collection at the 20th anniversary edition of Belgrade Fashion Week.

www.alexandramoura.com

1 spring summer 2007, *ModaLisboa - LisboaFashionWeek*
2 spring summer 2005, *ModaLisboa - LisboaFashionWeek*
3 spring summer 2006, *ModaLisboa - LisboaFashionWeek*

Photos: ModaLisboa Archiv, Rui Vasco

ANNHAGEN | COPENHAGEN
Dianna Opsund Bay

Born in 1974, creative director Dianna Opsund Bay founded the annhagen fashion company in 2004 and has already gained customers worldwide.
The collections are built around eloquent designs and dark nuances. The individual designs offer a detailed look with finely cut, sharp silhouettes. The style is avant-garde for everyday use, giving individuals a better opportunity to dress experimentally and creatively to produce a look that's as daring and raw as they feel. annhagen is a high fashion design label for the twilight hour – the time between a busy daily routine and the temptations of the night.

www.annhagen.com

1 fall winter 2007/08 collection
2 spring summer 2007 collection

Photos: Helle Moss (1), Dianna Nilsson (2)

ANN-SOFIE BACK | LONDON
Ann-Sofie Back

Originally from Sweden Ann-Sofie Back obtained a BA in Fashion Design from Beckman's College of Design in Stockholm. She moved to London and graduated with an MA in Fashion (Womenswear) from St Martins College of Art & Design in 1998. She worked for Joe Casely Hayford in London and various Swedish brands, combining this with the role of contributing fashion editor at Self Service and Purple magazines in Paris and Dazed & Confused in London.
October 2001 saw her debut Prêt-a-porter collection at the Purple Institute in Paris. After four seasons in Paris, she began showing at London Fashion Week. Her work has appeared in Vogue, i-D, W magazine, among others and at notable art museums and galleries. High profile stockists include Selfridges in London, Opening Ceremony in New York, and Midwest in Tokyo. In 2006 Back was asked to produce a capsule collection for Topshop. Following its success, T-shirt designs based around her past collections will be in the store for ss07.

www.annsofieback.com

1 fall winter 2004
2 spring summer 2004
3 spring summer 2006
4 fall winter 2006
5 spring summer 2007

Photos: courtesy of Ann-Sofie Back

4

ANTAEOS | BERLIN
Lisa Winkel

Lisa Winkel was born in 1978 in Finland. She trained in fashion design at the Universität der Künste in Berlin, where she studied under Vivienne Westwood, graduating in 2004. Among other projects and awards, she and her fellow Westwood graduates (Jessica Richard and Zsuzsana Kovacs) jointly won the Moet&Chandon Fashion Debut award in October 2005 with her label Emil & Sheikh.
In January 2006 Winkel launched her first Prêt-à-porter ready-to-wear collection (winter 06/07) under the name ANTAEOS, which was presented as part of the Hussein Chalayan Exhibition at Art Museum Wolfsburg. In July 2006 her spring/summer 2007 collection won her a finalist place in the BUNTE New Faces Award. Besides her ongoing collaboration with the Strickmanufaktur Zella GmbH in Thuringia, Winkel also works with the Institute of Natural Fibres in Posen. She is regularly heard on the radio as a fashion commentator, taking a tongue-in-cheek perspective of the latest fashion trends.

www.antaeos.com

1 fall winter 2006/07
2 spring summer 2007
3 fall winter 2007/08

Photos: Stefan Botev

1

2

ARTISTA | BUDAPEST
Nora Ràcz, Katalin Imre, Katalin Stampf, Edina Schön

Artista Studio was formed in Budapest in 1993 by six designers: Katalin Imre, Juli Ivan, Abel Köves, Nora Rácz, Edina Schön and Kati Stampf. From its inception the designers
wanted to create a unique mood / image, focusing on the
details of styling. Artista create bespoke 'one-off' designs
and make clothes to order in their own workshop.
However they also produce limited runs from the range
of designs through sub-contracted businesses. Artista has
hosted many fashion shows in Budapest and Vienna, which
have received wide media coverage. Activities have expanded into other creative areas such as film, commercial
styling, and event management. From 1998-2000 their ex-
pertise was used to develop a major Internet-based technology business for a UK company.

www.artistafashion.com

1 spring summer 2005
2 fall winter 2004 / 05
3 fall winter 2006 / 07

Photos: Hadley Kincade (1, 3), David Oszkò (2)

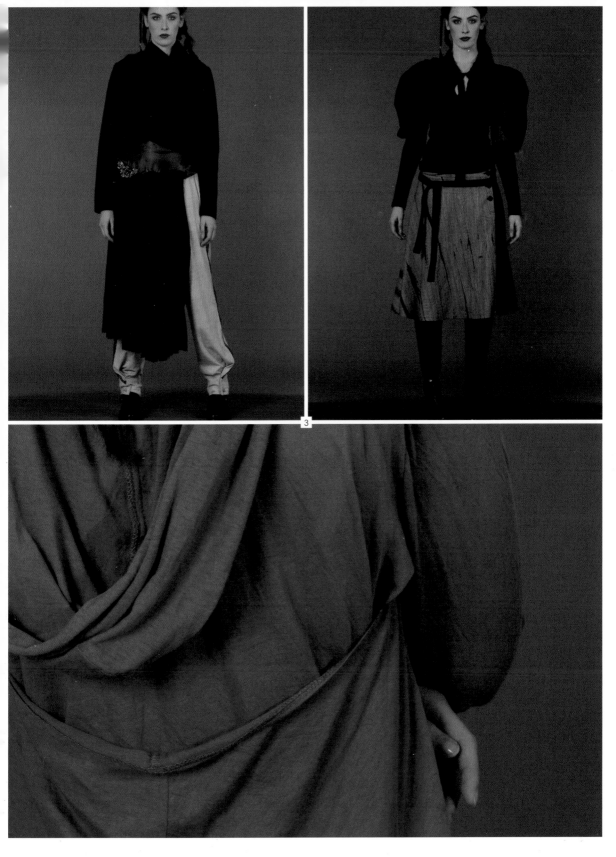

3

ATELIER GUSTAVO LINS | PARIS
Gustavo Lins

Born in Brazil, Gustavo Lins originally trained in architecture, completing his Masters at Polytechnique University Barcelona in 1989. He began freelancing as a pattern maker in 1990, working in womenswear for top industry names such as Jean-Charles de Castelbajac, Jean-Paul Gaultier, John Galliano, Kenzo Paris, and Agnès B; and in menswear, for Louis Vuitton and John Galliano since 2003.
He founded the brand Gustavolins in 2003 in order to develop a high fashion ready-to-wear collection for men and women. The collections have been distributed to selected stores such as Eclaireur (Paris), Maxfield (Los Angeles), The Library (London), Lift Etage (Tokyo), Jin (Seoul), and Dantone (Milan). Exhibitions and installations of his work have appeared at LIFT Etage, Tokyo; Gallery Joyce - Palais Royale and M+F Girbaud, Paris, among others.

www.gustavolins.com

spring summer 2007, *femme*

Photos: Michael Mohr

AVSH ALOM GUR | LONDON
Avsh Alom Gur

The London-based fashion designer graduated with distinction from the MA fashion course at Central Saint Martins
College of Art and Design. He was then recruited to Donna
Karan as evening wear designer for its mainline womenswear
collection. He has since engaged in freelance consultancy
projects for leading fashion houses such as Roberto Cavalli,
Chloe and Nicole Farhi before turning his attention to his
own fashion label, which was launched in 2005.
He has presented a catwalk show at London Fashion Week
for the past four seasons and received the Topshop and
British Fashion Council's New Generation Award for up-
and-coming designers over three successive seasons. His
collections challenge glamour and established definitions of
beauty, combining Eastern and Western elements with urban
street graffiti and underground grunge. In his design process
he regularly collaborates with emerging artists in jewelry
making, hand-carving, knitting, knotting and prints.

www.avshalomgur.com

1 spring summer 2007
2 fall winter 2007/08

Photos: Vanessa Ellis (portrait), Ian Gillett (1),
Niall McInerny (2)

1

2

AYZIT BOSTAN | MUNICH
Ayzit Bostan

Born in Ankara, Turkey in 1972, Ayzit Bostan moved to Germany in 1992 and studied fashion and technology at Munich Fashion School, having already completed an apprenticeship as a dressmaker. As a freelance dressmaker and fashion stylist she has undertaken costume design for a succession of commercials and feature films and in 1997 won the Munich City Award for Applied Arts.
The runway premiere of her ss2001 collection in Berlin (presented by Moet&Chandon and Vogue) was closely followed by the opening of her Berlin showroom. Her work has been widely published in magazines such as Elle, Frame and Domus, and featured in prominent exhibitions, including the Gallery Spruth Magers Projects and Gallery Gisela Capitain in Munich and Cologne in 1994, and more recently at the Goethe Institute in Tokyo in 2005.
Her 2007 collections have shown at Berlin Fashion Week and Rendez-Vous Paris.

www.ayzitbostan.com

1 fall winter 2006/07
2 spring summer 2007

Photos: Robin Roth (1), Oliver Spies (2)

1

2

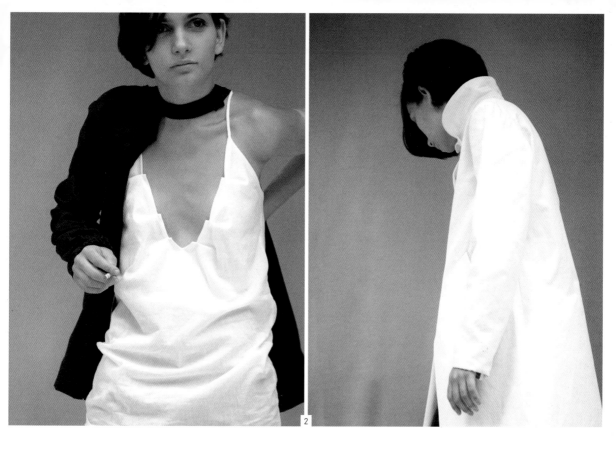

2

BAMBI BY LAURA | BARCELONA
Laura Figueras

Based in Barcelona, Laura Figueras studied at Winchester School of Arts, University of Southampton, then obtained BA Hons in Fashion at ESDI (Ramon Llull) Barcelona.
Bambi by Laura was founded in 2003 and produces two womenswear collections a year. Her work has been shown at Pasarel.la Barcelona (ss07), Circuit Lisbon Fashion Week (aw06/07), Tranoi, and Circuit Barcelona Fashion Week off-schedule shows (four consecutive seasons). She has also presented at Rendez-Vous Paris and Bread&Butter in Barcelona and Berlin.
Bambi by Laura has showrooms in France, London and Tokyo. Stockists include: Pineal Eye, London; Olga, Paris; and Dernier Cri, New York. Among various project commissions, she has created an exclusive press collection for the Absolut Label 2006 Project by Absolut Vodka; designed a Red Bull beachwear collection; and collaborated with Sex in Dallas (Berlin) on events and parties.

www.bambibylaura.com

1 spring summer 2007
2 fall winter 2006/07

Photos: Ugo Cámara (1), Nacho Alegre (portrait, 2)

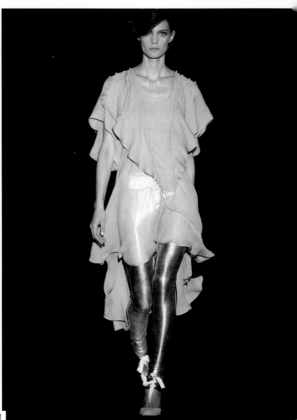

1

2

2

BOESSERT SCHORN | BERLIN
Sonia Boessert, Brigitte Schorn

Established in Berlin by Sonia Boessert and Brigitte Schorn in 2006, their collections are on continuous show in the Ideal showroom at Berlin Fashion Week, and with the dune agency at Tokyo Fashion Week. Both partners studied fashion design at Hochschule für Kunst und Design, Burg Giebichenstein in Halle, Germany from 1997-2002.

Since graduating they have participated in a number of shows and exhibitions, including Festival International des Arts de la Mode in Hyeres, France (2003); Selfware competition and exhibition in Graz, Austria (2003); Remode Platform for Art and Fashion in Vienna (2004); and the Becks Fashion Experience, Berlin (2005). The inspiration for the collections stems from craft and vintage, traditional costumes, clear/unclear material and colour, the everyday, the nonchalant, the contradictory.

www.boessert-schorn.de

1 fall winter 2006/07
2 summer 2007
3 fall winter 2007/08

Photos: boessert/schorn (1), Christian Netter (3), André Wunstorf (2)

2

2

3

BRUNO PIETERS | ANTWERP
Bruno Pieters

Belgian-born Bruno Pieters graduated with honours in fashion from the Royal Academy of Fine Arts Antwerp in 1999. He then worked as an assistant to Martin Margiela, Josephus Thimister and Christian Lacroix haute couture. In July 2001 he was the first graduate from Antwerp to present a couture collection during Paris couture week and described by Suzy Menkes as an intruiging new talent. The collection featured twelve silhouettes inspired by a 1950s newlook suit. French magazine l'officiel wrote, "Bruno Pieters made a fine debut probably the best couture presentation of the week."
Pieters launched his first ready-to-wear collection in March 2002. He is first and foremost a technician and a constructionist who likes to experiment with shape and proportion. In March 2006 he was photographed by Karl Lagerfeld for Madame Figaro magazine in a photoshoot that featured 30 of Paris's best designers. Pieters is currently also working for Europe's oldest leather goods house, Delvaux.

www.brunopieters.com

1 fall winter 2006/07
2 spring summer 2007

Photos: Marc Vonstein, Kris Van Damme, Etienne Tordoir (1), Sybille Walter (2)

1

2

C.NEEON | BERLIN
Doreen Schulz, Clara Leskovar

Based in Berlin, Clara Leskovar and Doreen Schulz graduated from Kunsthochschule Berlin Weissensee in 2004. The
label they co-founded - c.neeon - is an amalgamation of
their childhood nicknames. They won the prestigious Grand
Prix 2005 at the Hyeres International Festival and went on
to receive three awards from New Generation at London
Fashion Week, where they've shown their collections since
September 2005. In 2006 the Berlin 'Kunstgewerbemu-
seum' presented 30 to 40 'c.neeon' outfits together with
collages, videos and fotomontages in a solo 'c.neeon' exhibition.
The label first appeared in Berlin at the Beck´s Fashion Ex-
perience and at the Moet&Chandon Fashion Debut in 2004.
In 2005 they produced a special collection for Topshop.
The label is currently presenting its aw07/08 collection in
Shanghai, sponsored by VW.

www.cneeon.de

1 fall winter 2004/05, *Day dream nation*
2 fall winter 2006/07, *Haschmichmädchen*
3 spring summer 2006, *Do you remember the first time*

Photos: Alex Kohout (1, 3), Dune (2)

3

CHOUCROUTE | BERLIN
Troy Dabski

The German label CHOUcROUTE takes its title from the French name for sauerkraut and sausages, as well as its use as a nickname for German people. Troy Dabski, who founded his label in 2000 in Berlin, likes to live like a 'kraut' in Germany's capital.
As such, CHOUcROUTE is characterised by its unorthodox collections and presentations. Straight lines and rigorous cuts build unique shapes and forms while sharp contrasts underline certain tensions without losing the overall harmony. Dabski is inspired by music of all styles, from electronica to classical.

www.choucroute.de

1 spring summer 2005
2 fall winter 2005/06

Photos: courtesy of CHOUcROUTE

2

CHRISTOPH FROEHLICH | BERLIN, ANTWERP, LONDON
Christoph Froehlich

Born in Memmingen, Germany in 1978 Christoph Froehlich now lives in Italy and works at Diesel's creative department (menswear) as well as on his own collections. In 2005 he won a Diesel award enabling his own mini-collection to be launched in selected Diesel stores. He obtained his Master of Arts (fashion design) in 2005 from the Royal Academy of Antwerp and is a guest lecturer at the Academy of Fine Arts Basel. From 2001-2005 he assisted at shows in Paris for Dries van Noten among others.

He has since participated in numerous shows, including the Arhem Fashion Biennale 2007; Becks Fashion Experience 2006 in which he won an award for innovation in German design; and Salon Rendez-Vous Hommes 2006. Froehlich has also worked with various magazines such as KRANK-ZINE and FRONT – Belgian magazines for alternative film/illustration and contemporary art respectively.

www.christophfroehlich.de

fall winter 2006/07

Photos: Florian Schwarz

CONNI KAMINSKI | BRUSSELS
Conni Kaminski

The German-born designer has lived and worked in Brussels since 2000. Her debut collection was launched in winter 2005 and she now has clients in Japan, USA, Benelux, Germany, France, Sweden and Switzerland.
Kaminski completed an MA in Fashion Design at Hamburg Hochschule für Angewandte Wissenschaften then worked for womenswear fashion brand Uli Schneider from 1992 to 1998. In 1998 she won the Amica and Mustang Design Award. Kaminski's style is described as discreet and elegant with clever detailing and a sporty touch. Simple sophistication is achieved with light, flowing fabrics layered into asymmetric forms and often draped directly on the body. Production is undertaken in Belgium using high quality materials from France, Italy and Germany. She currently works with an agent in the Benelux and northern France and presents her collections twice yearly at international fashion fairs such as Rendez-Vous Paris, Premium + Berlin, and BFF-Brussels. Her creations have featured in stylish fashion magazines, including Peclers Paris and Sportswear International.

www.connikaminski.com

1 fall winter 2006/07
2 summer 2007

Photos: Dominique Deschacht (1), courtesy of Conni Kaminski (2)

1

2

2

DANIEL HERMAN | ZURICH
Daniel Herman

Born in 1972 Daniel Herman studied fashion design at Central St Martins College of Art and Design in London. Since then he has designed on a freelance basis for several prominent studios. In Paris he did work placements for John Galliano (1998) and Sharon Wauchob (1999); and in Japan he worked for Mikalady and Triumph in 2005. In 2000 he won the Swiss Textil Awards. He has been designing for Triumph International since 2003 on a freelance basis.

He has presented his collections at major shows in every important fashion city, including Milan, London, Salzburg, Moscow, Amsterdam, Osaka and Berlin.

www.danielherman.com

1 Daniel Herman für Triumph
2 fall winter 2006/07

Photos: Andrea Diglas (1), Christian Wiggert (2)

2

ELFENKLEID | VIENNA
Sandra Thaler, Annette Prechtl

Based in Vienna, for the last seven years designers Sandra Thaler and Annette Prechtl have been creating collections of simple and linear designs with clear forms and colors, placing emphasis on high quality and a timeless independence of seasonally changing trends. An unconventional mix of materials, cut and production techniques creates wearable yet unique clothing.

The brand is currently sold in Austria, China, Germany, Italy, Japan, Lebanon, UAE and USA. Both graduates from the Herbststrasse College for Fashion and Garment Production in Vienna, their first ever collection, Tirol, won the Pierre Lang Fashion Award. In 2003 they opened a store and studio in Vienna. Their work continues to be presented at national and international conventions, exhibitions, and events including Rendez-Vous in Paris and Inside White in Milan.

www.elfenkleid.com

1 fall winter 2007/08
2 spring summer 2007, *fashion show*

Photos: Joerg Auzinger

1

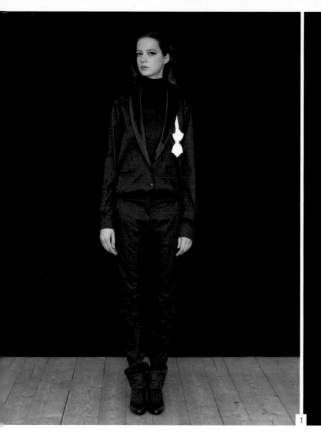

1

2

ELUISE | COPENHAGEN
Louise Stubkjær Sørensen

Louise Stubkjær Sørensen graduated from Kolding Design
School in 2001. Based in Copenhagen, Denmark, her vision
for Eluise is ambitious; bravely and uncompromisingly avoid-
ing indifferent trends and commercial dictations. For ss07
she has reinterpreted voluminous sculptural silhouettes
with references to the casual and also the controlled.
Classical aesthetic clarity combined with controversial details creates modern elegance with subtle undertones of
the avant-garde. Her fascination with contrasts and decon-
structed tailoring is clearly evident while exclusive materials and a tight colour scheme complete the picture.

www.eluise.dk

spring summer 2007

Photos: Noam Griegst

EVA GRONBACH | BERLIN, COLOGNE
Eva Gronbach

The German designer, who lives and works in Cologne and Berlin, sets topical issues in a new fashion context with her creations, thus inspiring fresh agendas for debate. She enjoys observing how fashion is able to alter people's perceptions. After five years' study at La Cambre in Brussels and Institut Francais de la Mode (IFM), Paris, she received her Diploma and MA. Eva Gronbach has worked for Yohji Yamamoto (Paris), Stephen Jones and John Galliano (Paris/ London), and at Hermes (Paris).
She first caused a stir on the international fashion scene with her collection 2000 'Déclaration d'amour à l'Allemagne'. In 2007 she established her new casual wear brand "german jeans" which is based on vintage coal miners' clothes. Her clothes are sold in Europe, USA and Japan.

www.evagronbach.com

1 fall winter 2007/08
2 german jeans

Photos: Boris Breuer (portrait), Sylvie Tillmann (1, 2)

FRIEDA DEGEYTER | BRUGGE
Frieda Degeyter

Having graduated from the fashion department at Antwerp
Royal Academy of Fine Arts in 1993, Belgian designer Frieda Degeyter worked for several commercial labels before
launching her own children's collection in 1999.
Its styling is unique and unlike any of the conventional
children's wear brands in Belgium or overseas. In 2001 she
expanded by introducing her first womenswear collection.
Drawing on inspiration from travel and architecture, the
designs are distinguished by a strong and inventive colour
palette of fresh fabrics and prints.

www.friedadegeyter.com

1 fall winter 2001/02
2 spring summer 2005

Photos: Roger Dickmans (1), Bert Houbrechts (2)

2

GASPARD YURKIEVICH | PARIS
Gaspard Yurkievich

Born in Paris in 1972, Yurkievich's collections have been gracing the catwalks since 1998. Besides regular exposure at 'Pret-a-porter', his creations have appeared at fashion shows in New York, Tokyo, Singapore, Zurich and Sao Paulo. He completed his studies at Studio Bercot in 1993, gaining work placements in the studios of Jean Paul Gaultier and Thierry Mugle.
He has since designed collections for renowned labels such as Prisunic/Monoprix and La Redoute, and has garnered top awards from competitions including the 12th International Festival of Art and Fashion at Hyères (1997), and ANDAM (1998). Yurkievich's work has featured in prominent exhibitions, notably Les Plus de la Mode at Musee des Art Decoratifs in 1998, where his designs sat alongside those of John Galliano, Comme des Garcons and Martine Sitbon.

www.gaspardyurkievich.com

1 spring summer 2007 men
2 spring summer 2007 women
3 fall winter 2006/07 women

Photos: Shoji Fujii

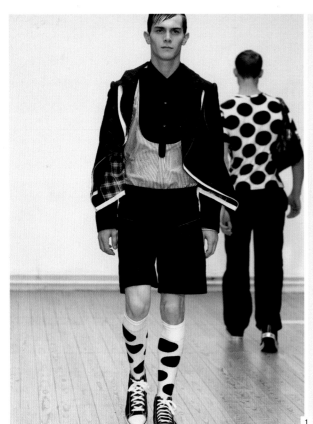

1

2

2

3

GEOFFREY B. SMALL | CAVARZERE VENEZIA
Geoffrey B. Small

Geoffrey B. Small has continuously worked to raise the art and sciance of making individualized clothes by hand. He founded the Area Paris show to serve the needs of independent designers, and has pioneered many design trends including recycle fashion design, designer streetwear, Napoleonic-era style and his radical new medieval direction.
He believes that great clothes and the people and techniques behind them should be valucd far more highly, and that financial and marketing considerations, together with short-term business interests, are becoming far too dominant in fashion. On the contrary, he insists that fashion is an art, and must be used to raise design quality—not lower it, speak the truth about the world—not lie about it, and do its best to help make life better for everyone—not just an elite few.

www.geoffreybsmall.net

1 Paris fashion show 2007, „*Classe Dirigeant*"
2 Venice Film festival 2005, *clothes for Veruschka*
3 Paris fashion show 2007, *"Heroes of another gender"*
4 Paris fashion show 2006, *"Ode to Toussaint Louverture"*
5 Paris fashion show 2006, *"Waves of Fear"*

Photos: Guido Barbagelata

2

3

HALL OHARA | LONDON
Yurika Ohara, Steven Hall

The Japanese designer Yurika Ohara was born in 1979 and studied at the Vantan Design Institute in Tokyo, receiving Distinction on the international course, Foundation Studies in Art & Design (1998-1999). In 1999 she joined the BTEC Diploma Foundation in Art & Design programme at the London College of Fashion, passing with Distinction in 2000. She completed her training at Central St Martins College of Art & Design in London from 2000-2003, where she obtained a First Class BA (hons) in Fashion Design Womenswear.
Born in 1980, the British designer Steven Hall began his training at the London College of Fashion in 1997, obtaining a Distinction in BTEC ND in Fashion Design and Textiles. He subsequently completed a BTEC Diploma Foundation in Art & Design in 2000, also with Distinction. In 2000, Hall attended Central Saint Martins College of Art & Design, graduating with a First Class BA (hons) in Fashion Design Womenswear in 2003.
The Hall Ohara fashion company was launched in 2005 at London Fashion Week and appeared there in its exhibition and on the catwalk. The brand also featured at Paris Fashion Week, exhibiting at Rendez-Vous Femme aw06/07 and at ZipZone ss07. Industry accolades include Topshop's New Generation Award for ss06.

www.hallohara.com

1 fall winter 2006/07
2 spring summer 2006
3 spring summer 2007

Photos: Kyoko Homma

2

2

3

HALTBAR | MUNICH
Kathleen Waibel, Peter König

Born in 1969 in Tettnang, Germany, Kathleen Waibel trained in fashion design from 1993-1998 at the College of Design, Basel (Switzerland). She has since undertaken costume design for theatre productions in Vienna, Munich, Hamburg, Freiburg and Zurich as well as for several short films. More recently her role expanded to include styling for commercial films and photo productions. In 2001 Waibel co-founded the product design label HALTBAR with Carmen Boch, Alexa Frueh and Peter Koenig, unveiling their first collection in September 2001 at Andreas Murkudis, Berlin, and subsequently at Vitra Design Museum (Basel), Berlin Designforum and Roomservice (Hamburg) among others.

The HALTBAR MURKUDIS brand was established in 2003, encompassing two unisex collections a year. Waibel currently lectures at the Institute of Fashion Design, HGK - University of Design and Art, Basel and in 2007 launched the label HALTBAR KATHLEEN WAIBEL with Peter König.

www.haltbar.de

1 fall winter 2003/04, *first collection in design collaboration with Kostas Murkudis*
2 fall winter 2003/04
3 fall winter 2007/08, *men's collection*

Photos: Thomas Degen (1), Judith Buss (2), Markus Jans (3)

1

3

HARTMANN NORDENHOLZ | VIENNA
Filip Fiska, Agnes Schorer

The fashion label was founded in 2000 by designers Filip Fiska and Agnes Schorer, who met while studying at the University of Applied Arts in Vienna, Austria. Born in Tübingen, Germany, Schorer studied under the direction of Marc Bohan, Helmut Lang and Jean-Charles de Castelbajac. Fiska was born in Vienna, Austria and trained with Jean-Charles de Castelbajac, Viktor & Rolf and Raf Simons.
Their collections convey generous silhouettes and a contemporary attitude combined with classical couture traditions. With their profound knowledge of tailoring they try to redefine "occasional clothing" to give every occasion meaning, importance and adequate allure without losing a touch of playful irony. In 2002 they were the winners of the Austrian Fashion Award for contemporary design.

www.hartmannnordenholz.com

1 spring summer 2007, *circus*
2 spring summer 2006, *toll*
3 fall winter 2006/07, *luxus*
4 fall winter 2005/06, *gedenken*

Photos: Nordenholz

1

1

2

2

4

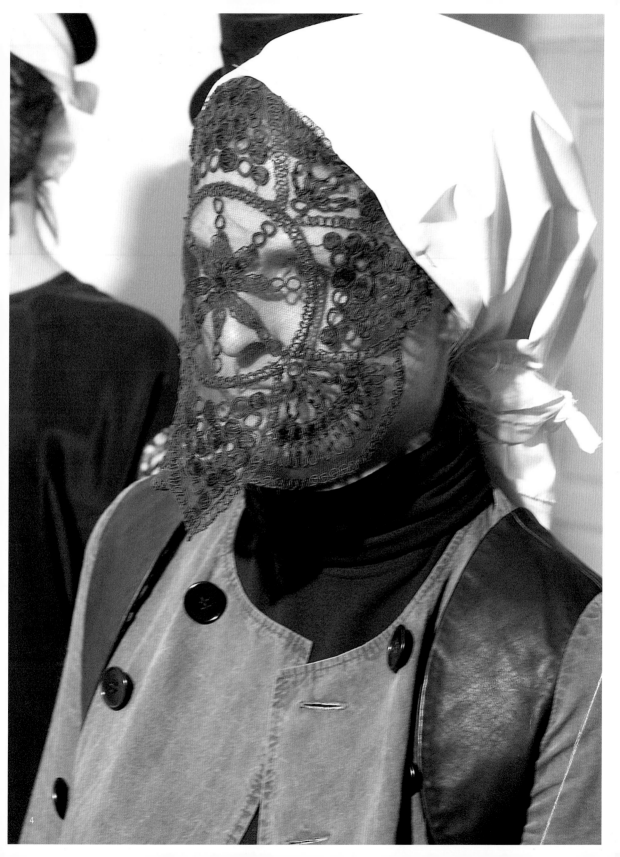

HENRIK VIBSKOV | COPENHAGEN
Henrik Vibscov

Born in Denmark, Henrik Vibskov's creative input to the visual arts, film and music dates back several years. He has owned his fashion label in Copenhagen since 2001.

Vibskov's work questions existing shapes, while often referencing traditional tailoring. His creations have captured interest from the fashion scene worldwide and are sold in selected stores including Colette Paris, Mads Nørgaard Copenhagen, Midwest Tokyo, and Penelope Italy.

He is the only Scandinavian menswear designer on the official catwalk list in Paris, alongside such prominent names as Givenchy and Dior. Since graduating from Central Saint Martins College of Art and Design in 2001, press coverage (in magazines such as The Face, Dazed and Confused, I-D, Wallpaper, and Vogue) has been constant. His work has also featured in numerous exhibitions, appearing at Midwest Tokyo, Factory Tokyo, ICA London, Sotheby Gallery New York, Palais de Tokyo Paris, V1 Gallery Copenhagen, and Hyeres Festival France among others.

www.henrikvibskov.com

fall winter collection show 2007/08, *The black carrots*

Photos: Jacob Langvad (portrait), Shoji Fujii

JAIN CLOSE MARC SZWAJCER | ANTWERP
Jain Close, Marc Szwajcer

Jain Close and Marc Szwajcer first presented their collab-
orative work in 2005. Jain began working in 1999 under her
own name in Melbourne, Australia. Over the next few years
she received continual recognition before relocating to
Antwerp in 2004.
Having graduated from the Faculty of Social, Political and
Economical Sciences, Brussels University, Marc Szwajcer
undertook fieldwork in West Africa and Madagascar before
venturing into documentary making, publishing and visual
anthropology.

www.jcms.be

1 fall winter 2006/07
2 spring summer 2007

Photos: courtesy of UNION NV/SA

JEAN-PIERRE BRAGANZA | LONDON
Jean-Pierre Braganza

In 2002 Braganza graduated with a First Class BA (hons) in Womenswear from Central Saint Martins College in London, winning the Colin Barnes Award for Illustration and participating in the press catwalk show at York Hall, London. He was subsequently taken on as designer at Roland Mouret, London. In 2004 his debut collections were presented at London Fashion Week, aw04/05 and ss05. The latter was also presented in Osaka, Japan alongside other international desigers.

The creation of his ss06 collection was televised in December 2004 as part of an ITV documentary series, Big Night. Braganza's following collections have been prominently featured in successive London Fashion Week shows, including aw05/06 titled Testamental and aw06/07 titled Subtyrannical, which both appeared in the On|Off exhibitions at The Royal Academy, London. Braganza continues to present his collections at London Fashion Week every season to critical acclaim.

www.jeanpierrebraganza.com

1 spring summer 2006
2 spring summer 2005
3 fall winter 2005/06

Photos: Ian Gillet

3

KAVIAR GAUCHE | BERLIN
Alexandra Fischer-Roehler, Johanna Kühl

The fashion label was founded in 2004 by Johanna Kühl and Alexandra Fischer-Roehler who both completed their diploma in fashion design at ESMOD International School in Berlin. Swedish-German and born in 1980, Kühl worked as a pattern-cutter and design assistant at Jenny Hellstrom in 2000 before undertaking an internship at Vivienne Westwood's studios in 2002, later joining Martine Sitbon as design assistant in 2003.

Alexandra Fischer-Roehler was born in Germany in 1975 and began her career in fashion/music/trends publishing and advertising. She became a finalist at the Moet&Chandon Fashion Debut in 2003 with her first 'Pret-a-porter' collection.

They were nominated for the Swiss Textiles Award in 2006 and won the visionary award On|Off the same year.

www.kaviargauche.com

1 Advertisement print media 2006
2 Advertisement print media summer 2007
3 spring summer 2007, *catwalk*

Photos: Frauke Fischer (portrait), Andrej Glusgold (1), Norbert Bäres (2), Moore Photography London (3)

1

2

3

KOSTAS MURKUDIS | BERLIN
Kostas Murkudis

Born in Dresden and of Greek decent, Kostas Murkudis now lives and works in Berlin. After graduating from the pretigious Lette Verein School of Fashion in Berlin he worked with Helmut Lang for seven years. In 1996 he formed his own company in Munich and debuted in Paris with his women's wear spring/summer collection in 1997. Besides working on his own men's and women' wear label, he joined the italian brand 'New York Industries' and was their creative director from 2000-2003. In 2005 he first launched 'Schiesser - Kostas Murkudis' men's and women's wear.

www.kostasmurkudis.net

1 fall winter 2000, women
2 in collaboration with hellenic fabrics 2000
3 spring summer 2001 men, *école des beaux arts, Paris*

Photos: Jork Weissmann

KRISTIAN AADNEVIK | LONDON
Kristian Aadnevik

The 29 year old Norwegian has an MA from London's Royal College of Art (2002) and a background in tailoring. He set up his own label in 2004. His collections border on couture but have a dark edge, contrasting volume and embellishment with sharp tailoring, slim cut silhouettes and refined detailing using the finest materials. During his studies at the RCA he won several awards and worked as a design assistant for Alexander McQueen. Aadnevik has designed collections for several respected international labels including Charles Jourdan Paris where he had the role of chief designer for the Japanese market.

www.kristianaadnevik.com

1 spring summer 2007
2 spring summer 2006

Photos: Tomas Falmer/ESP (2), Christopher Moore (2, p. 222-223), Mikael Schulz/Soderberg Agentur (1)

1

1

KRISTIN HENSEL | HALLE/SAALE
Kristin Hensel

Born in Leipzig in 1979, Kristin Hensel studied Fashion Design at the University of Art & Design Burg Giebichenstein Halle (Saale), German, graduating in 2004. She assisted at the Vienna-based designer labels Eva Blut and Wendy&Jim before establishing her own label the same year.
Her collections have since been presented at various prominent shows and exhibitions, including the Beck's Fashion Experience in Berlin (2005), Ideal Showroom Berlin during Berlin Fashion Week, Rendez-Vous Femme at Paris Fashion Week (2005), and Go Asia - Artist in Residence/Kunststiftung des Landes Sachsen-Anhalt (2006).

www.kristinhensel.com

1 fall winter 2005/06, *Things Around Me*
2 spring summer 2006, *The Inner Circle*

Photos: Andreas Bartsch

2

226

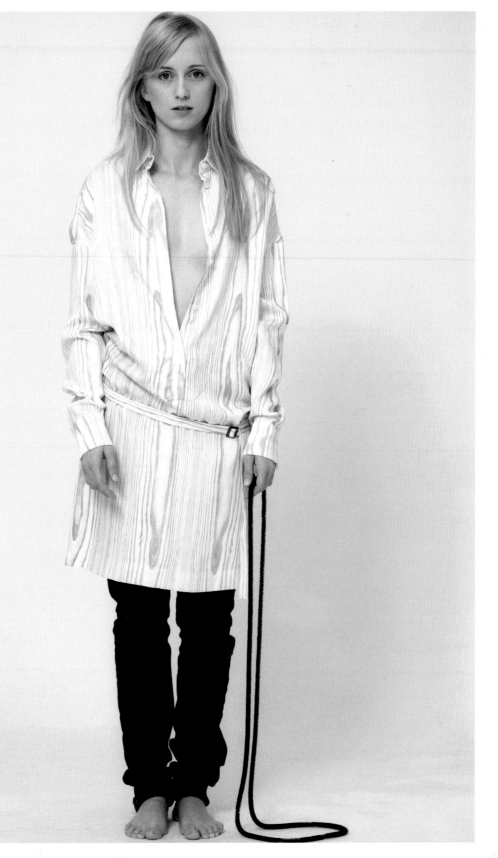

L GABRIELE KOCH | COLOGNE
Gabriele Koch

Born in 1963 in Hagen, Germany, Gabriele Koch initially trained in Language Studies in France before attending Law School in Bochum, graduating in 1987. In 1991 her career changed direction when she began studying dressmaking. By 1994 she had completed her final examinations at the Fashion School Schloß Eller Düsseldorf, and was presented with the Fashion Future Award and the Young Design Fashion Award.

Koch subsequently worked as a freelance fashion designer and in 1995 was admitted to the Kreativhaus Düsseldorf IGEDO. In the same year she won the Fashion Design prize Northrhine Westphalia. From 1996-2002 she was engaged in costume design for various dance productions in Cologne. During this time she took part at the International Fashion Design Award Berlin Brandenburg (1997) and won the Cologne Dance Prize (1999). In 2006 she established her own label L Gabriele Koch.

www.gabriele-koch.com

L soir 2007

Photos: Joannis Golias

LUDVÍK | COLOGNE
Fenja Ludwig

German designer Fenja Ludwig initially studied and mastered the art of tailoring before undertaking a degree in fashion design. She had a vision when she founded her label Ludvík in 2003 and simultaneously opened her own small boutique in Cologne. Her vision proposes a new interpretation of the traditions of dressmakers at the haute couture houses in Paris through the help of modern and contemporary pop culture. Only with the highest accuracy of manufacturing processes and technical precision is it possible to achieve such aesthetic perfection.
Her collections are designed to accent the figure and amplify every personality with an emphasis on elegance and sportive chic.

www.ludvik-cologne.de

1 fall winter 2006
2 spring summer 2007

Photos: Gabriel Dimanos

1

LUTZ | PARIS
Lutz Huelle, David Ballu

Founded by Lutz Huelle and David Ballu, the women's ready-to-wear collections are designed from their studio in Paris and sold in selected stores across Europe and in Japan, China, Australia and USA. With a first class degree in fashion design from London's Central Saint Martins College, Huelle then spent three years working with Martin Margiela. Ballu was previously with Cosmopolitan Cosmetics where he was responsible for special events worldwide. He has worked for Jean Paul Gaultier and ALAÏA, and currently consults to a French retail chain.

In 2004 Huelle was invited to the GWAND Festival of Fashion and won the 'Ackermann' 'Prêt-a-Porter Prize'. Lutz collections have featured in many exhibitions, most notably at Museum fur Kunstgeschichte (Cologne), Musée de la Mode et du Textile (Paris), and Fonds Regional d'Art Contemporain (Reims) which showed a retrospective of the first 10 collections in 2004.

www.lutzparis.com

fall winter 2007/08

Photos: Wolfgang Tillmans (portrait), Petrov Ahner

MARCEL OSTERTAG | MUNICH
Marcel Ostertag

Born in Berchtesgaden, Marcel Ostertag trained at Central St Martins College, London obtaining a BA(hons) in 2004 for which he was awarded first prize for the best menswear collection. He stayed to complete an MA in Fashion Design Menswear, graduating in 2006. While studying, he undertook numerous ventures, including projects with Paul Smith, Dunhill and Burberry. He subsequently presented his work at the Lancome Colour Award and at the Victoria and Albert Museum in London, being the first menswear designer to have received this privilege.

Ostertag's style is unique and irrepressible. He interprets classic menswear in a manner that allows masculine and feminine characteristics to come together in an exciting symbiosis. This results form a harmony between elaborate detail and clear, precise tailoring. The opening of his first store in Vienna (October 2006) was closely followed by the second store opening in Munich. He is currently considering further projects in London and Shanghai.

www.marcelostertag.com

collection 2006

Photos: courtesy of Marcel Ostertag

MELODIE WOLF | PARIS
Melodie Wolf

The Paris-born designer studied at Studio Bercot, which led to a host of work with industry names such as Mafia Agency, Kenzo and Andre Walker. Following the successful launch of her accessories line, Wolf gave birth to her first full collection, presenting it during the Autumn/Winter 2004-05 Paris fashion season.

Since then, her focus has moved toward knitwear, exploring pattern and fulfilling a passion for jacquards, but also for volumes, drapes and pleats. An eclecticism and thirst for inspiration – whether from American Golden Age musicals or Russian ballets – have enriched her collections. From perfectly executed handmade knitwear to macramé, printed jersey, skin and crocheted pieces, her designs have a personal, distinctive touch that has slowly evolved through mastering her own techniques and production methods.

www.melodiewolf.com

1 fall winter 2006/07, *underwood*
2 spring summer 2006, *secret stairs*

Photos: Kai Jünemann (portrait), Shojii (1, p. 242, 2), Tania et Vincent (1, p. 244)

1

2

MINIMARKET | STOCKHOLM
Sofie Elvestedt, Pernilla Elvestedt and Jennifer Elvestedt

Minimarket is a Swedish clothing brand established by three sisters: Sofie, Pernilla and Jennifer Elvestedt. The trio was selected by Swedish Elle and H&M as best new designer label of the year, 2006. The design philosophy is based on using opposites to create perfect balance, combining sensual, comfortable appeal with a touch of extravagance.

The three sisters have widely varying tastes and styles, so it's the challenge of finding a unifying path in design that inspires the group. Sofie's sense of style is well-groomed and feminine, Jennifer's is more masculine and street-style in attitude, while Pernilla prefers rock'n roll chic and draping techniques.

www.minimarket.se

1 fall winter 2007/08
2 spring summer 2007
3 fall winter 2006/07

Photos: Peter Gehrke/Adamsky (1), Andreas Larsson/Adamsky (2, 3)

MONIKA DRÁPALOVÁ | PRAGUE
Monika Drápalová

For nearly 10 years Monika Drápalová has been creating 'Pret-a-porter' collections under the fashion brand Modra, with distribution reaching France, Belgium, UK, Italy, Holland as well as Japan, USA and Lebanon. She trained in fashion design at the Academy of Decorative Arts Prague, from 1990-1996. Her first studio opened in Prague in 1998, and the second in 2001 in Lyon, France.

Her "Collection 2000" was awarded first prize in the Camif competition (Prague-Paris). She has twice won the title "Designer of the Season" – at Prague Fashion Week. In 2004 she won the Printemps store competition in Lyon. Her work appeared at the International fashion fair 'Prêt-à-Porter' Paris from 2001-2003 and at the Luxury Trade Show in Paris in 2006. She had her own fashion show at the Royale Gallery, Paris in 2003, and presented her collection at the Czech Bene-Fashion, Milk studios, New York in 2006.

Over the years she has undertaken costume design for theatre and cinema, advertising campaigns such as T-Mobile, Nescafe, Levis etc. and collaborated with jewellery producers and other fashion labels. From 2003-2006 she was fashion designer of the couture collection Korloff Paris.

www.modra-fashion.cz

1 spring summer 2007
2 spring summer 2007, *fashion show PFW*
3 fall winter 2006/07, *Magazine Dolce Vita*

Photos: Anna Kovačič (1, 3), Martin Zeman (2)

1

NADINE MOELLENKAMP | DUSSELDORF
Nadine Moellenkamp

Born in Dusseldorf, Germany in 1976, Nadine Moellenkamp gained a dressmaking aprrenticeship in 2001 and
subsequently studied at the Fashion Department, Royal
Academy of Fine Arts, Hogeschhool Antwerp, Belgium. She
graduated in 2006 and undertook internships at the Diesel
Style Office, Italy and at Victor & Rolf, Amsterdam. During
her studies she assisted backstage at the fashion shows
of Dries van Noten and Veronique Branquinho. Successes
include winning first prize at the cpd Dusseldorf 'Design am
Rhein' fashion project, and receiving the Becks Fashion Experience Design Award in 2007.

www.nadinemoellenkamp.com

Spring summer 2006, *concat*

Photos: Marleen Daniels

NOIR | COPENHAGEN
Peter Ingwersen

Peter Ingwersen is the mastermind behind the NOIR fashion label. He was previously employed as Brand Manager for Levi's RED and LEVI's Vintage before moving on to become Managing Director at Day, Birger et Mikkelsen, the internationally renowned Danish clothing brand.
Ingwersen wants Noir to be the brand that makes corporate social responsibility sexy. The collections are designed to respond to both consumer fashion and social conscience, with the aim of creating meaningfulness in the luxury segment.

www.noir-illuminati2.com

spring summer 2007, *nihil sine illumina*

Photos: Marc Høm

Patrik Söder

PATRIK SÖDERSTAM | STOCKHOLM
Patrik Söderstam

Patrik Söderstam is defined by a need to express feelings in a progressive and innovative way. These are visualised through clothing design, photography, graphics, styling and art works, all undertaken by Söderstam personally.
The label does not exist to earn money, perform as a business or please the customer. Instead, his designs have generated work for other companies such as Nike, Nokia and Absolut Vodka. This is the philosophy of the company. His clothes, photography and graphic work are featured in magazines such as Dazed and Confused, i-D, GQ and Arena Homme+, and seen in videos from the likes of Madonna and others.

www.patriksoderstam.com

1 fall winter 2006, *I woke up*
2 spring summer 2006, *The SOD*
3 fall winter 2004/05, *TV*

Photos: Patrik Söderstam

PENKOV | BERLIN
Bernadett Penkov

Bernadett Penkov graduated from Esmod Berlin in 2002 and received the Prix Createur Esmod for the best diploma collection. She won prizes at ITSone and Hempel China Fashion Award.

After working for Gilles Rosier in Paris for a while, Penkov decided that Berlin was far more inspiring and she returned there to launch her own label. It proved to be the right decision for Penkov - Berlin's broad creative scene offered more opportunities to create something new, unlike the established fashion industry in Paris.

In 2003 the project under the name MaisonAnti was established with a partner. But after one succesful year it was time to go one's own way.

In 2005 penkov is founded and is now sold in Europe, Japan and the United States. In October 2006 Bernadett Penkov won the Moet Chandon Fashion Debut 2006 and is now showing her collection in Berlin, Milan and Paris regularly.

www.penkovberlin.com

1 fall winter 2007/08
2 fall winter 2006/07

Photos: Wiebke Bosse (1), Florian Kolmer (2)

1

PETER BERTSCH | ANTWERP
Peter Bertsch

Born in Cologne in 1979, Peter Bertsch now resides in Antwerp, Belgium. He trained at the Royal Academy of Arts in
Antwerp, graduating in 2006.
During his studies he participated in a number of fashion
projects, producing designs for his "Yaroslav" Menswear
collection (2004), his "I love" Womenswear collection
(2005), the Orchid hat project with Elvis Pompilio (2006)
and the "Headphone" prototype for Louis Vuitton in 2005.
He was chief editor of the magazine "+One", a collaboration with 17 belgian fashion designers, which was sold out
worldwide (2007). In 2007 he won with his graduation Collection "bionic" the Anne-Chapelle-prize "createur" and the
Becks Fashion Award in Berlin.

peterbertsch@yahoo.de

1 Bionic 2004
2 I love 2005
3 Yaroslav

Photos: Ronald Stoops (1, p. 290, 293), Willy Cuylits (1),
courtesy of Peter Bertsch (2, p. 294), Etienne Tordoir (2),
Jean l'Oliviere (3)

1

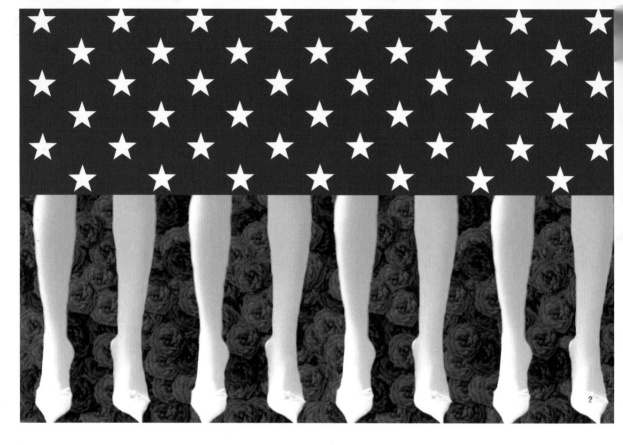

2

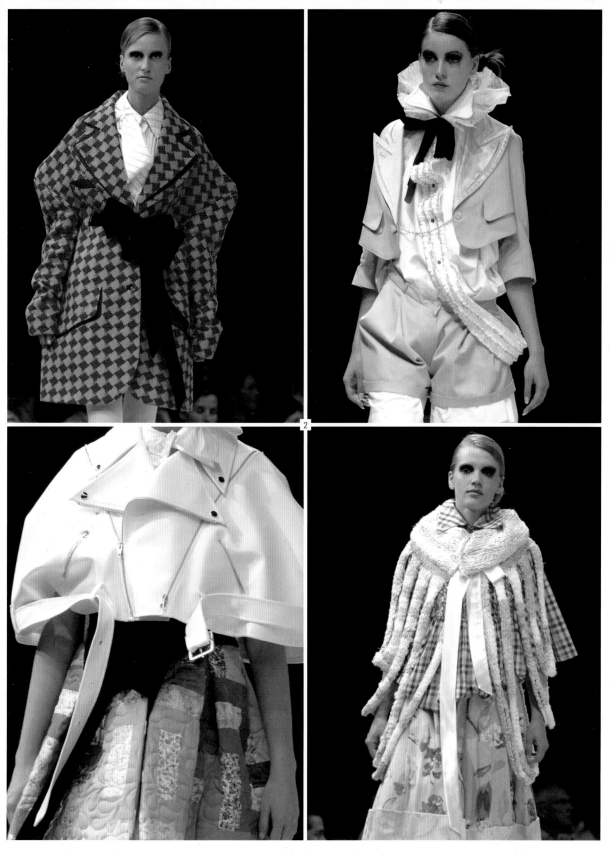

PETER PILOTTO | ANTWERP
Peter Pilotto

Born in 1977, the Austrian designer studied art and fashion in London before working as a window dresser at Vivienne Westwood for three years. From 2000-2004 he trained at the Royal Academy of Fine Arts, Antwerp. His graduation collection was distinguished by the Flanders Fashion Institute. Other accolades include the Coccodrillo Shoe Award, Maria Luisa Award and Unit F Award. Moonlight shadow is a recurring theme for Pilotto, forming a material surface that signals the future from a time in the past. His designs are poetic, avant-garde and elegant, embodying a play of identities that defy explanation and convey a magical appeal.

The video installation of his graduation collection has been widely exhibited, debuting at the 'Window Gallery' of Walter Van Beirendonck, Antwerp in 2004; then showing at the Centre Cultural di Andratx under curator Yilmaz Dziewior of Kunstverein Hamburg; also at the Museum Boijmans Van Beuningen, Rotterdam; and as a video documentation at the Fashion Video Presentation in the Centre Culturel Suisse, Paris. His work regularly features in fashion magazines such as Elle, I-d and Women's Wear Daily.

www.peterpilotto.com

1 fall winter 2006/07
2 spring summer 2007

Photos: Bruna Kazinoti (portrait), Pieter Huybrechts, Ellen Smeets

2

POSTWEILER HAUBER | EPPELHEIM/HEIDELBERG
Raphael Hauber

Founded in August 2003 by German designers Eva Postweiler and Raphael Hauber, they both studied fashion design at the HFG Pforzheim, Germany, graduating in 2003 as
best-of-class and best student respectively. The label's first
collection was launched in Paris alongside the aw04/05
Prêt-à-porter womenswear shows and their ss05 collection
featured as an internet presentation during women's fashion week in Paris. Their work was subsequently shown at
men's fashion week in Paris (February and July 2005), Hauber now directs the brand solely and collections are mixed,
for both men and women.
In January 2006 the aw06/07 collection 'Der Blaue Reiter'
was presented in Paris and at Ideal in Berlin as a runway
show. The ss07 collection appeared in Paris during men's
fashion week again and in Berlin at Bread & Butter Studio in
July 2006. POSTWEILER HAUBER is regularly featured in I-d,
Dazed & Confused Japan, Arena Homme, among others.

www.postweilerhauber.com

1 fall winter 2007/08, *collection "Completed"*
2 spring summer 2006, *collection "The night in your mind"*
3 fall winter 2005/06, *collection "Where the sky is so blue"*

Photos: Heinz-Peter Knes (portrait), courtesy of Postweiler
Hauber

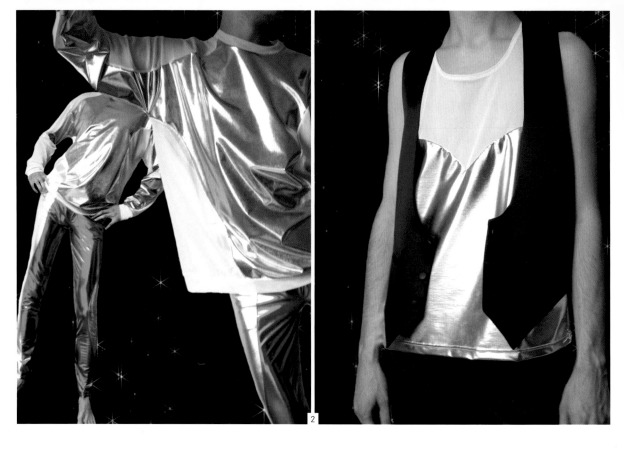

2

PULVER | BERLIN

Elisabeth Schotte, Franziska Schreiber, Therese Pfeil,
Franziska Piefke

The Berlin-based studio unites effortlessly elegant style
with elaborate cut and detail, taking a conceptual, innovative approach to each collection. The design process is ac-
companied by research and the concept is often inspired
by a fictional or real person. Founded in 2003 by Elisabeth
Schotte, Franziska Schreiber, Therese Pfeil and Franziska
Piefke, the Pulver style is influenced by their respective experiences while working for designers Hussein Chalayan,
Rubin Chapelle, Cynthia Rowley, and Nigel Curtiss. Schreiber received the graduate award of the FHTW Berlin and
the Lucky Strike Junior Designer Award 2003.
Working as a team of four designers forms both the core and
the point of departure for their collections. Pulver garnered
the Bread&Butter Foundation Award in 2003, which led to
their first collection. Since then the collections – which are
produced in Germany – have been developed twice yearly
and are sold in Germany, Japan, Hong Kong and the USA.

www.pulver-studio.de

1 fall winter 2007/08
2 spring summer 2007
3 fall winter 2005/06

Photos: Özgür Albayrak (1), Markus Jans (2), Iris Janke (3)

3

Q.E.D. | BERLIN
Julia Böge, Simona Gabrieli, Jasmin Moallim

q.uod e.rat d.emonstrandum, shortened to q.e.d, is a Berlin-based fashion label founded by Julia Böge, Simona Gabrieli and Jasmin Moallim. The German designers all graduated from fashion school in 2006 and began working on their first collection, 'Jerry Lewis vs. Kasparov' shortly afterwards.
The garments are very wearable yet exquisitely detailed and subtly avant-garde. Their debut collection emerged on the runway in January 2007 at the Becks Fashion Experience, where q.e.d. was selected as the only menswear collection - among the field of designers participating - to represent the best in young German design talent. In the same month, their work was also exhibited at the Ideal showroom in Café Moskau.

www.qed-homme.com

1 fall winter 2006/07

Photos: Jana Denzler

RAEBURN DESIGN | LONDON
Christopher Raeburn, Graeme Raeburn

Raeburn Design is the unique partnership of brothers Christopher and Graeme. Focusing on functional beauty in the 21st century cityscape, they have produced collections inspired by modern, nomadic lifestyles and clothing for extreme weather conditions. Both graduates from London's Royal College of Art Womenswear Masters Degree, their work has always been highlighted for its exquisite attention to detail, progressive cutting and ethically intelligent design.

www.raeburndesign.co.uk

1 spring summer 2004, *Fashion Fringe*
2 spring summer 2003, *A reason for Beauty*
3 fall winter 2007, *Godspeed*

Photos: Royal College of Art catwalk show (2), Mike Blackett (1, 3)

3

3

SPASTOR | BARCELONA
Sergio Pastor Salcedo, Ismael Alcaina Guerrero

Spastor - founded by Sergio Pastor Salcedo (Girona 1975) and Ismael Alcaina Guerrero (Barcelona 1975) - launched their debut men's collection in 2004. Since then they have created fashion shows and presentations for press and customers at Paris' men's Fashion Week, Barcelona's Fashion Week and Madrid's Pasarela Cibeles. Spastor has worked with several photographers, including Marcelo Krasilcic who photographed Spastor's debut show in Paris. Among other events, they conceived the soundtrack for artist Joan Morey's work DOMINION, and have taken part in projects such as DESIGNERS AGAINST AIDS directed by Ninette Murk, and in Spanish government exhibitions such as 12 TRAJES PARA TOKYO. Their garments have been worn by Marilyn Manson and lauded by other artists such as The Kills, Rammstein, The Horrors and Patrick Wolf. Spastor is currently designing clothes for a contemporary dance piece by Rafael Bonachela.

www.spastor.org

1 spring summer 2007
2 fall winter 2006/07
3 spring summer 2006

Photos: Daniel Riera (portrait), Biel Sol (1), Spastor (drawing, 2), Wade H. Grimbly (3)

1

2

3

TILLMANN LAUTERBACH | PARIS
Tillmann Lauterbach

Born in 1977, Tillmann Lauterbach spent the first seven years of his life in Ibiza, Spain. He then returned to Germany and at fifteen moved to Switzerland. He joined Deutsche Bank as a trainee, but also became involved with modeling and various artistic projects for brands, such as Marie Claire, GQ, Uomo, Paul Smith, Levis, and Lacoste.
In 2000 he switched profession and entered the renowned Esmod Fashion College in Paris, graduating two years later with a diploma as a patterncutter and designer, garnering the award for best final degree women's collection. In the same year, 2003, he joined plein sud in Paris as an assistant designer. Other projects include the Cocoon Club in Frankfurt.

www.tillmannlauterbach.com

1 spring summer 2007
2 fall winter 2006/07

Photos: Fabian Frinzel (portrait), Richard Jensen

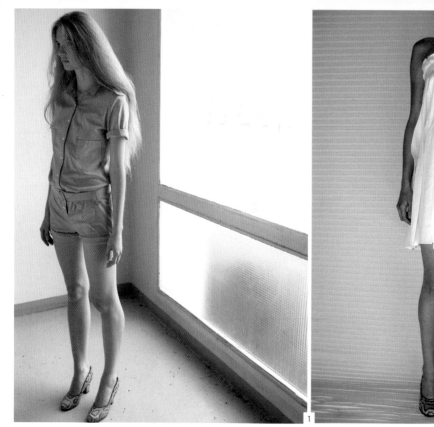
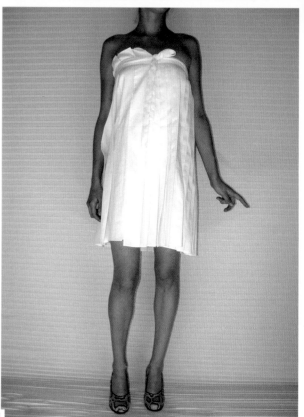

1

TONJA ZELLER | HAMBURG
Tonja Zeller

The Hamburg-based designer studied at University Hoch-schule für Angewandte Wissenschaften (Hamburg), completing a fashion design diploma in 2005. Her work has appeared in a succession of international fashion award events, including the Becks Fashion Experience in Berlin (2004), ITS TWO in Triest (finalist, 2003), ONWARD in Tokyo (prize for workmanship, 2002), and GWAND in Luzern (student joint first prize, 2001). Zeller's debut collection under her own label was launched for the Autumn/Winter 2006-07 season with the help of Company 1.2.3. This was presented at the 21st Festival International de Mode et de Photographie in Hyeres in 2006, where she had won the Prix 1.2.3 the year before.

www.tonjazeller.com

1 fall winter 2006/07
2 fall winter 2007/08

Photos: Estelle Hanania (portrait), Grégoire Alexandre (1, p. 346), Shoji Fujii (1), Ulrich Diehl (2)

2

TXELL MIRAS | BARCELONA
Txell Miras, designer of Neil Barrett's womenswear

Born in Barcelona in 1976, Txell Miras established her own creative brand in 2003 and has been designing for Neil Barrett women's wear ever since. She graduated in Fine Arts from University of Barcelona in 1999 and launched her debut exhibition at Belles Arts gallery the same year. She continued her studies in Fashion Design at the Llotja Arts School of Barcelona, winning first prize in Milan's Domus Academy competition 'Insideouting' in 2001.

In 2002 she received her Master's from the Fashion Domus Academy. She was awarded best young designer of the Barcelona Fashion Week and in 2003 co-awarded most promising young designer of Italiy by the Camera de la Moda Italiana. Her background in fine arts is the key to appreciating Miras's unique style – she seeks inspiration from across all artistic fields including cinema, painting, sculpture, music and literature. In 2006 she received the "Barcelona es moda" Award and was selected to represent Spain in the European Young Fashion Summit (Vienna).

www.txellmiras.eu

1 fall winter 2003/04
2 fall winter 2006/07
3 spring summer 2007

Photos: Jordi Solé (1), Passarel·la Barcelona (2, 3)

1

1

2

UEG | WARSAW
Ania Kuczynska, Michał Łojewski

Michał Łojewski was born in 1974 in Warsaw. He spent his childhood in Tokyo before returning to Poland to attend the Secondary School of Fine Art. He subsequently graduated with an MA in Graphic Design from the Academy of Fine Arts in Warsaw, where he also studied Industrial Design. He describes himself as a die-hard minimalist, adhering to the maxim 'less is more'. He eschews colour in favour of monochrome, and avoids trends or literal reinterpretation.

In 1996 he founded the Warsaw-based White Cat Studio which specializes in corporate identity, packaging and brand design. He is also co-founder of the anti-fashion label UEG, established in 2003 with Polish fashion designer Ania Kuczynska. This gave him the opportunity to merge art with packaging and fashion. He is Art and Design Director of FUTU magazine, and co-founder of STGU association of designers.

www.ueg.pl

1 2006, *lifestyle packaging*
2 2007, *love*

Photos: Artur Wesolowski (1), Marek Straszewski (2)

1

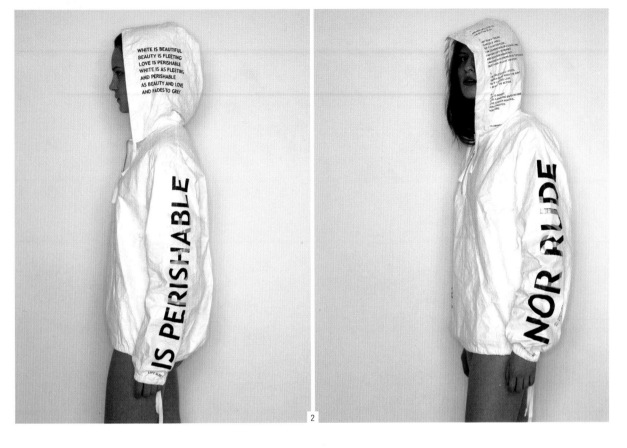

2

UTE PLOIER | VIENNA
Ute Ploier

Vienna-based Ute Ploier established her menswear label in 2003. January 2004 marked her debut in Paris when her aw04/05 collection was shown at the UCAD during Paris Fashion Week. She has since shown two collections per year and the brand is sold in selected stores in Europe, USA and Japan. Her creations reflect a critical view, blending humour and irony with respect to the images and expectations of masculinity that clothing builds, expresses, and deflates.

Born in Linz (Austria) in 1976, after one year in London attending fashion and graphic design programmes at Central Saint Martins College, she attended the University of Applied Arts, Department of Fashion, Vienna in 1996 where she was taught by Jean-Charles Castelbajac, Viktor&Rolf and Raf Simons. In 2000, while still at University, she presented her first collections in Vienna and Berlin. In 2003, she was awarded the renowned Prix Hommes for best menswear collection in Hyères, France.

www.uteploier.com

1 fall winter 2005/06
2 fall winter 2006/07

Photos: Bernd Preiml (1), Shoji Fujii (2)

XUAN-THU NGUYEN | PARIS
Xuan-Thu Nguyen

The Dutch fashion brand was established in 2001 and has a loyal following all over the world, from Tokyo to New York, Milan and Madrid. Nguyen's first boutique opened in Le Marais, Paris in 2004. Her creations mix modern geometric pleats with delicate and fragile accents such as handmade embroidery.

Because of the simplicity of finishing and invisible cutting techniques, the designs are not only this season but also next. The designer undertakes a continual search for new methodologies that will enhance the concealed stitching and finishing so that nothing detracts from the garment's design.

www.xuan-thunguyen.com

1 spring summer 2005, *Out of Place*
2 fall winter 2004/05, *In your Voice*
3 fall winter 2006/07, *Outline*

Photos: Karin Nussbaumer (v1, 3), Jo van den Assem (2)

2

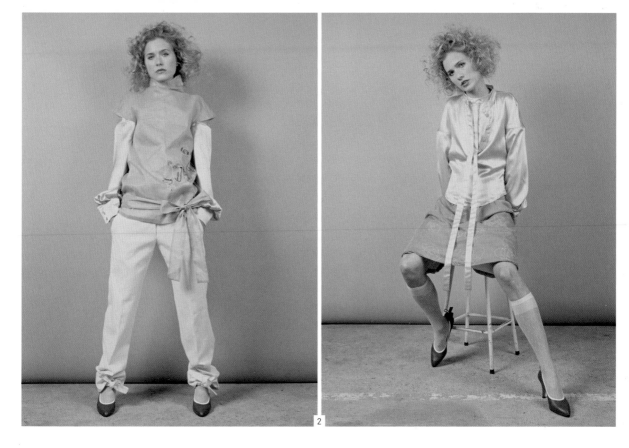

2

INDEX

© 2007 daab
cologne   london   new york

published and distributed worldwide by
daab gmbh
friesenstr. 50
d-50670 köln

p + 49 - 221 - 913 927 0
f + 49 - 221 - 913 927 20

mail@daab-online.com
www.daab-online.com

publisher ralf daab
rdaab@daab-online.com

creative director feyyaz
mail@feyyaz.com

editorial project by fusion publishing gmbh stuttgart . los angeles
© 2007 fusion publishing, www.fusion-publishing.com

editor christine bierhals
editorial assistance katharina feuer

layout katharina feuer
imaging jan hausberg, martin herterich

photo credits
coverphoto helle moss, backcover dune
introduction page 7 sybille walter, 9 anna kovačič, 11 ronald stoops, 13 mikael sculz,
15 grégoire alexandre
editor biographies anna koor
text introduction christine bierhals
translations by ade team übersetzungen/stuttgart, claudia ade
english translation jill kaiser
french translation jocelyne abarca
spanish translation sara costa-sengera
italian translation paola bassoli

printed in italy
www.zanardi.it

isbn 978-3-86654-013-2